Pueblo Spirits
in the life of
Felicitas D. Goodman

Susan G. Josephson

Copyright © 2014 Susan G. Josephson
zsuzsjosephson@gmail.com

All rights reserved. No part of the contents of this book may be reproduced in any form without the written permission of the publisher.

Righttree Digital, LLC
3335 Johnson St. NE
Minneapolis, MN
55418

publish@righttreedigital.com

Contents

Preface 4
Escape 5
Lion Spirits 16
Spider 36
Death 48
About The Author 70

Preface

Pueblo Spirits is a true story of spirit encounters in the badlands of New Mexico. It is based on the life of the internationally known anthropologist Dr. Felicitas D. Goodman.

When Dr. Felicitas Goodman (Felix) was about to retire from teaching linguistics and anthropology at a college in Ohio, she decided to buy 273 acres of New Mexican badlands. There were ruins of ancient pueblos on the property, and she thought that made it perfect for an anthropologists' retirement. She did not know about the spirit shrine on the land. Several people had encounters with spirits there, but although she was eager to have an experience herself, nothing happened. She was warned about the dangers, but she became obsessed with contacting those spirits. That obsession drove her research until she finally discovered trance postures that open channels to the spirit world. She founded Cuyamungue institute (now called the "Felicitas D. Goodman Institute." (www.cuyamungueinstitute.com) and wrote books and articles and gave workshops about her discoveries. Then finally the spirits took notice of her. She discovered her true name but nearly lost her life.

Felix is my mother. Before she died in 2005, she authorized this version of her life story. Her only conditions were that I point out that names have been changed, disparate events have been made simultaneous, and separate people have been rolled together into a single character. Felix discusses some of these events in her books: *Where the Spirits Ride the Winds*, and *My Last 40 days*, (both Indiana University Press).

Escape

Pueblo Spirits

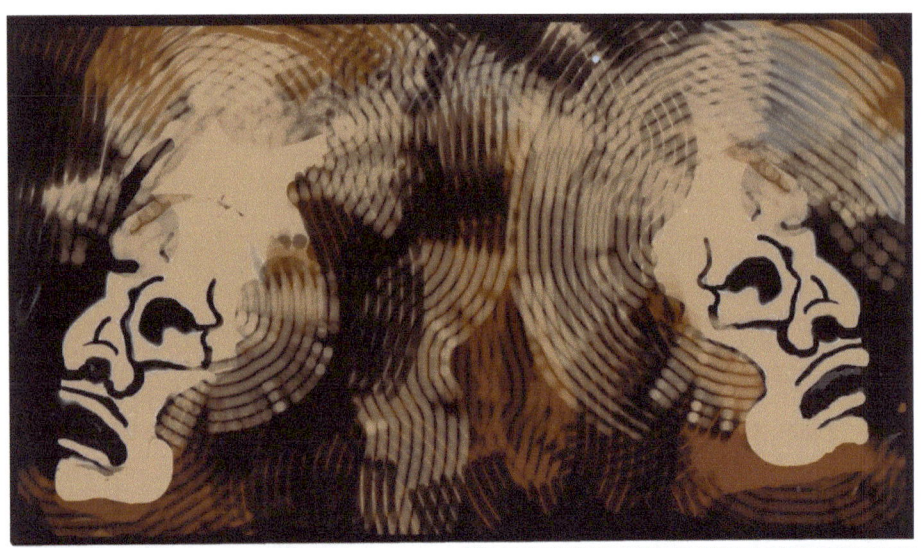

"WHAT DID YOU SEE?"

"I WAS IN THE TENT WHEN AN ANIMAL SHAPE WENT BY. THEN IT WAS INSIDE THE TENT. IT HAD BLACK HOLES FOR EYES AND MANY TEETH. THEN IT WAS GONE."

Lion Spirits

Pueblo Spirits | 18

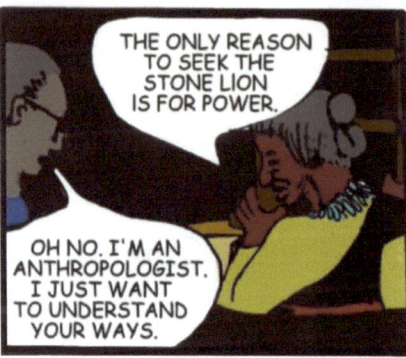

Spider

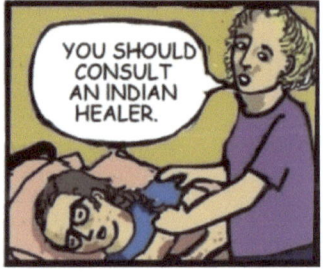

WHEN I WAS FEELING BETTER WE DID A TRANCE TO DETERMINE COSTUMES AND RITUALS.

JOAN WAS SHOWN A YELLOW BIRD AND I WAS SHOWN A BUFFALO.

I WONDERED WHY A BUFFALO?

WE DANCED AROUND THE POLE.

THE TRANCE BEGAN.

Death

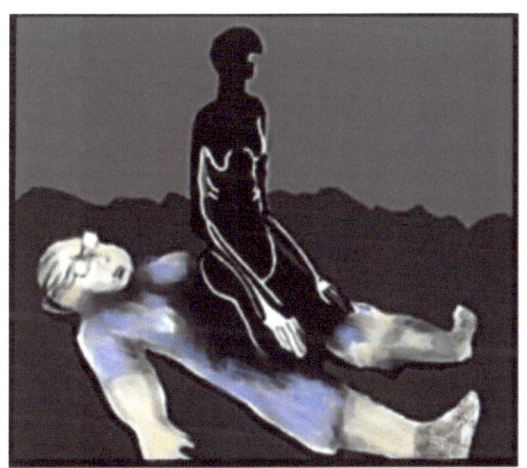

THE END

About The Author

Susan Josephson has a husband and two grown sons and three grandchildren and an old black cat. She has a Ph.D. in philosophy from The Ohio State University and was a professor of philosophy at Columbus College of Art and Design until she retired in 2011. She has written books and articles on artificial intelligence and art and illustrated several books, including *My Last Forty Days, A Visionary Journey among the Pueblo Spirits*, by Felicitas D. Goodman, Indiana University Press and *The Ecstatic Experience, Healing Postures for Spirit Journeys* by Belinda Gore, Bear and Company.